MOROCCO

MOROCCO

Photographs
by
Dorothy Hales Gary

Text by
Lord Kinross

A Studio Book
The Viking Press · New York

First published in 1971 by The Viking Press, Inc.
625 Madison Avenue, New York, N.Y. 10022

Published simultaneously in Canada by
The Macmillan Company of Canada Limited

SBN   670–48956–5

Library of Congress catalog card number: 79–135346

Printed and bound in Switzerland

Of the lands of North Africa, the Arabs have a saying: "Algeria is a man, Tunisia a woman, Morocco a lion." Morocco is certainly a lion of a country, if ever there was one. Together the three lands form what has been called the Fourth Shore of Europe. Algeria and Tunisia do indeed complement its main shores. Known to the Arabs as Ifriqiya (in corruption of the Latin "Africa") and running horizontally from west to east, they form together a "peninsula" of mountainous coast-line, striking out toward Sicily between two seas—the Mediterranean and an ocean of sand, the Sahara.

Morocco, on the other hand, tilts diagonally from north-east to south-west, looking in part towards Europe but belonging in essence to Africa and to the Atlantic Ocean. It is a country in depth, spreading far into the continent before it meets the Sahara, reaching out as close to America as the most westerly coast-line of Europe. Morocco is the Far West, in a sense still the Wild West, of the North African world. In Arabic it is known as the Maghrib, the Land of the Sunset.

It is a land scored by great ranges of mountains, with broad plains between. There are four of these ranges. To the north, like a wall along the Mediterranean, are the mountains of the Rif, geologically an extension of the mountains of Andalusia, in the Spanish peninsula. Running right across the centre of the country, from north-east to south-west, is the great ridge of the Middle Atlas, which separates north from south. Beyond it is the High Atlas, and beyond that again the Anti-Atlas, looking south to the Sahara.

Morocco's geography has conditioned its history. Because of its mountainous interior and of its inhospitable Atlantic seaboard, it has always been a country hard to conquer and, once conquered, hard to control. Tunisia was always easily enough dominated and colonized, both from the east and

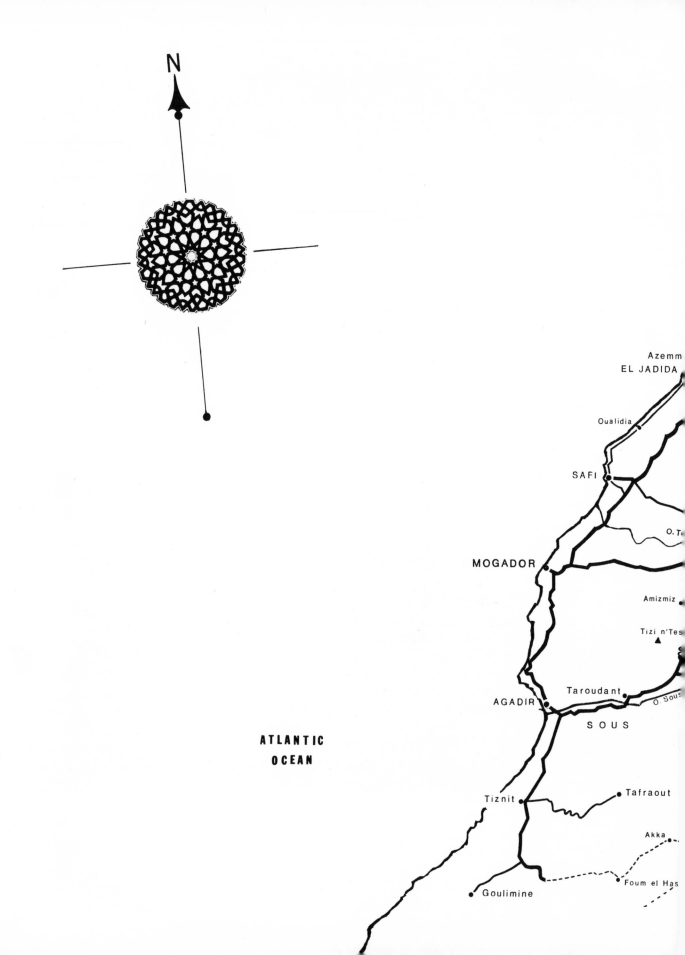

N

Azemm
EL JADIDA

Oualidia

SAFI

O. T

MOGADOR

Amizmiz

Tizi n'Tes ▲

Taroudant

AGADIR   O. Sous

SOUS

ATLANTIC
OCEAN

Tiznit   Tafraout

Akka

Foum el Has

Goulimine

from Europe—successively by the Phoenicians, the Romans, the Vandals, the Byzantine Greeks, the Arabs, the Turks. Not so Morocco. The Phoenicians stuck to the coast-line. So, a thousand years or so later, did the Portuguese. The Roman occupation, unlike that of Tunisia, was partial and limited in character, being confined only to parts of the north. The Vandals and the Byzantines barely touched it. The Turks never asserted effective control over it.

The Arabs invaded Morocco in the seventh century, as they had invaded the rest of North Africa, but at first treated it largely as a springboard for the invasion of Spain. In later invasions, as people of the plains, they hardly penetrated into the mountains or across them. Nor were they as destructive as they had been throughout Ifriqiya. Eventually they established throughout the land an Islamic society whose culture and institutions and language were Arabic. It became known as Mauretania, a name that the Romans had given to part of it, and its inhabitants as Mauri, or Moors. It gave to Morocco a sense of identity as a country which Tunisia and the other North African lands never achieved. But its racial and political roots were not primarily Arabic. They were Berber. For Morocco is essentially the land of the Berbers, the indigenous race whom the Greeks and the Romans called the Barbarians. It is, in fact, Barbary.

The Berbers are an ethnic group of cryptic origins, which has been established in the Mediterranean basin for many thousands of years. Emerging, it is thought, from the Middle East, they seem originally to have been a white race, as some of them—the veiled, blue-eyed Tuareg of the Sahara—still are. But with the passage of time and the mixture of strains, the Berbers have progressively darkened in complexion and embrace today a variety of physical types. They are united, however, by a common Berber language, which is said to have links with both the Semitic and the ancient Egyptian, and is still spoken by three million Moroccans.

They are united, too, by a common character, a fierce sense of independence embodied in the name, which—conversely to that of barbarism—means the "free and noble spirit." The Berbers were always a fighting race. They served as mercenaries in the armies of the Carthaginians. As Strabo describes them, "they fight for the most part on horseback, with a javelin; and ride on the bare back of the horse, with bridles made of rushes. They have also swords. The foot soldiers present against the enemy, as shields, the

Inside Andalusian Mosque facing minaret door, Fez

ABOVE: Ritualistic washing of hands and feet; 'Attarin Medersa, Fez. RIGHT: Almohad ramparts, twelfth century, Marrakesh

ABOVE AND OPPOSITE: Street scene in the wool-dyers' quarter, Fez

OPPOSITE: A small pottery in the Souk, Marrakesh. ABOVE: Berber women near Telouet

Colorful headdress at village wedding, near Telouet

skins of elephants. They wear the skins of lions, panthers, and bears, and sleep in them." They were a populous, vigorous African race who, in Strabo's time, lived largely as nomads—hence the Roman name of Numidia, for the present Algeria. "They bestow care," he wrote, "to improve their looks by plaiting their hair, trimming their beards, by wearing golden ornaments, cleaning their teeth, and paring their nails; and you would rarely see them touch one another as they walk, lest they should disturb the arrangement of their hair."

There are nomads among them still, chiefly in the wide desert regions. But in the mountains and plains they are composed largely of settled village communities. A tribal people, fighting as often with each other as against the foreigner, they are united in no national sense but by a common social structure. Each Berber group has its own customs, but all share a similar organized system of government, and this is in essence self-government, based on democratic or oligarchic traditions and allowing a voice in affairs to each villager, each tribesman within the community. The Berbers form, in fact, a confederation, or series of federations, of small and independent tribal republics, loosely affiliated on a kind of cantonal basis; and herein lies their strength.

It lies also in their religion. Following the Arab invasion, the Berbers were quick to embrace Islam, and to evolve their own forms of it. They became in a sense more Moslem than the Moslems. They produced Berber holy men, Berber saints, Berber prophets, Berber Messiahs, a whole series of separate Berber cults—at one point even a separate Berber Koran. They outdid the Arabs in their worship of marabouts, holy men with their individual shrines. The general trend of these movements was Nonconformist, Puritanical—what in Christian terms would be called today "Low Church." The Berbers had revivalists among them. They had mystics. Their beliefs and practices reverted to the purity and austerity of the earlier days of Islam, to the days of the Prophet Mohammed himself in the Arabian desert, before the Arabs, in the course of their imperial progress, became prone to be influenced by the corrupt tendencies of the outside world. These religious forces, as the history of Morocco unfolded, gave political power and strength to a sequence of some six ruling dynasties, over a period of a thousand years, which were predominantly Berber in origin. Morocco evolved a growing and flourishing civilization which was, in its essence, a compound of Berber and Arab.

The face of Morocco has been compared picturesquely to a harlequin's cloak. Geographically, ethnologically, socially, it is, of all the lands of the "Arab world," the most diverse. Today communications and centralized government are drawing the country together. But a decade or so ago there were relatively few Moroccans who could be said to know Morocco as such. In the bare black mountains of the Sarro, beyond the Atlas, there were tribes of so-called Moroccans unaware that such a country existed. The Berbers knew their mountains, the Arabs their plains, the Berbero-Arabs their own parts of both. The sardine fisherman knew his Atlantic harbours, the Saharan nomad his desert tracks and markets, the townsman the streets and buildings of his growing modern cities. But few of these Moroccans knew much of each other. For a generation the French strove, in a paternalist protectorate, to bring these component parts together. So, in their own regions, did the Spaniards. Today the Moroccans themselves strive to do so, in the person of a powerful though constitutional monarch, King Hassan II, following his ancestors of the Alawite dynasty. But for the traveller Morocco remains a land of infinite variety, in terms of landscape and buildings and people.

Symbolizing this variety, in historical terms, are the contrasting civilizations of Rome and Islam as seen, dramatically side by side, in the classical city of Volubilis and the adjacent Moslem holy city of Moulay Idris. The Roman occupation of Morocco was sketchy and brief compared to that of Tunisia, which was developed on a large commercial scale for agricultural settlement and the production of grain for Rome itself.

At first the Romans ruled this Moroccan region indirectly, through two Berber satellite kingdoms, Mauretania and Numidia—régimes comparable to those of the French and Spanish protectorates two thousand years later. Mauretania's capital was Volubilis, where, about 25 B.C., it had an enlightened, serious-minded ruler in a Berber named Juba, appointed King of Mauretania by Augustus Caesar. Punic in name—an abbreviation of Jubal, or "Glory of Baal"—and Punic in culture, Juba was brought as a young man to Rome, where he was given a first-class Greco-Roman education. Roman sources describe him as "the most historically minded of all Kings." He amassed a large library, containing a number of Punic books, and himself wrote or compiled in Greek some fifty works dealing not only with history but with geography and such scientific subjects as botany. One of these described a plant, a species of spurge, found in the Atlas Mountains, which he called after his doctor, Euphorbia. Pliny records that its milky juice was found to be an aid to clear sight, hence a remedy for conjunctivitis—a service-able medicament for these parts, where eye diseases have always abounded. It was used also as an antidote against snake bite and poisons of all kinds. It became so popular with the Berber tribesmen that they diluted it with goats' milk to make it go further.

Juba also established a successful industry, probably at Mogador, on the Atlantic coast, for the manufacture of a purple dye from shellfish. This became the imperial purple of Rome, and a great source of wealth for his dynasty. But it led the dynasty to ultimate disaster. Juba had married the daughter of Antony and Cleopatra, who was named Cleopatra Silene, the Moon, while her brother was named Helios, the Sun. They had a son named Ptolemy, who succeeded him as King. Summoned in A.D. 41 by his cousin, the mad, bad Emperor Caligula, to attend him on a visit to Lyons, Ptolemy appeared in the Roman amphitheatre arrayed in the finest of purple cloaks. This won him an ovation from the assembled crowd. The Emperor, driven mad with jealousy, at once had him secretly executed. Caligula himself was assassinated a year later. But "by his cruelty," as Pliny puts it, he suppressed the autonomous Berber kingdom. Mauretania was annexed to the Empire as a Roman province and divided into two by his successor, the Emperor Claudius—provoking a serious revolt which it took a large Roman army three years to suppress.

Juba seems to have maintained a court of some sophistication. A man of taste as well as of learning, he was a discerning connoisseur of works of art, and a fine collection of early bronzes, which date from his time, was un-earthed at Volubilis. Founded as the capital of his Berber kingdom, it now became the seat of government of the western Roman province. Spaciously built, over a fertile plain at the base of a limestone range which provided stone for its construction, Volubilis is the only notable Roman ruin to be seen in Morocco, a country which seems, from the absence of classical cities and of paved Roman roads such as abound in Tunisia, to have been relatively lightly held and to have been undeveloped in Roman times. This is, however, a substantial colonial city, with traces of a surrounding wall, built to protect it against the incursions of the rebellious Berber tribes, who continued to give trouble.

Elsewhere in the province there is evidence of camps and other lines of fortification, some doubled with underground passageways, to facilitate defence. Consuls and generals of the time were fond of boasting to Rome how they had penetrated the Middle Atlas in pursuit of these natives and had routed them. But Strabo is inclined to be sceptical as to how far they actually succeeded in doing so.

Like many a traditional Roman city in Europe, Volubilis boasts a spacious forum, with a handsome basilica and capitol, and a broad colonnaded street culminating in a triumphal arch of Caracalla. It was in effect a garrison town, as its large number of ruined villas, of varying degrees of opulence, indicate. Built along three main streets, with the Governor's palace at the end, they have such evocative names as the House of the Horseman, of the Deer, of the Nereids, of the Bathing Nymphs, of the Jumping Athlete, of the Labours of Hercules, and they contain fragments of mosaic pavement which illustrate their several subjects. In the House of the Cortège of Venus, for example, the goddess was portrayed riding the waves (a mosaic now in the Tangier museum), while Diana may be seen bathing naked with her nymphs. Bacchus is flanked by the Four Seasons, and the beautiful young Hylas, the companion of Hercules, is abducted by other nymphs during the voyage of the Argonauts.

These houses of Volubilis were furnished with such amenities as heat and water. The House of Orpheus has traces of a central-heating system, fired by a furnace, which warmed the rooms through terra-cotta vents in the walls and beneath the floors—floors adorned in mosaic with a version of the Orpheus myth, with dolphins frolicking in the waves in the company of sea-horses, crustacea, and several varieties of fish. It is equipped with its own bathhouse, similar on a private scale to the public baths of Gallienus nearby. Here a series of elaborate installations provided rooms with four grades of temperature from hot to cold—*caldarium, laconicum, tepidarium, frigidarium* —a blessing for the inhabitants of so dusty a country. Finally Volubilis shows evidence of Roman industrial enterprise: oil refineries, equipped with a system of presses; mills, drainage channels, and basins for the production and storage of oil from the olive trees then cultivated in the surrounding countryside.

The classical art of Volubilis, with its lively pagan mosaics, depends on free portrayal of the human face and form. This was strictly prohibited by Islam, the civilization which after a few centuries filled the gap left in Morocco by the decline and fall of Rome. Henceforward the art of the country, decorative in style as it is, rich in colour and inventive in design, is confined to the wholly abstract patterns of the Moslem artistic tradition.

20

Never again, throughout Morocco, does the traveller see a human scene portrayed.

Across the plain from Volubilis, stepping steeply up twin hills, is its direct antithesis, the small, whitewashed Arab town of Moulay Idris, for more than a thousand years a shrine of Moslem pilgrimage. Dominating it, closed to the infidel, is the green-roofed tomb of the much revered holy man whose name it bears. Moulay Idris, a direct descendant of the Prophet Mohammed through his daughter Fatima, reached Walila—as the Arabs called Volubilis—towards the end of the eighth century, as a fugitive, with his followers, from the forces of Harun al-Rashid. Well received by the local Berbers, he established, with the aid of a coalition of Berber tribesmen, Morocco's first great Moslem dynasty, which was to last for some two hundred years. Finding himself hampered by shortage of water at Volubilis, where the country had dried up following the decline of Rome and its subsequent neglect, Idris shifted his headquarters to a more fertile and at the same time more strategic site, on the left bank of the river at Fez.

Here Harun al-Rashid had him poisoned by his agents, as a rebel and heretic, with a form of tooth-paste which he was induced to apply to his gums as a cure for a toothache. He was succeeded by a posthumous son born to a Berber woman, Moulay Idris II, who moved his capital across to the right bank of the river. The two cities started as rivals, with a wall between them, but eventually, in the early ninth century, grew into one, the great city of Fez as it is today. Water was plentiful, refreshing the city through a system of conduits and cisterns and fountains and watermills, which evolved through the centuries and still survive. For Fez was long to outlive the dynasty of its founders and to grow into a great medieval city of culture and learning, given new life from the eleventh century onwards by an influx of Moslems, returning to Morocco from Spain. This was to give it a Spanish feeling, diluting the more austere atmosphere of the Islamic cities farther east.

Fez is still a medieval city, contained within walls, with great battlemented gates and closed to all wheeled traffic. It is thus a city exclusively for pedestrians, two-footed or four-footed, so that the traveller walks—or rides—through it everywhere, and sees much of it as it must always have been. For when the French took over Morocco in 1912, Marshal Lyautey, the enlightened "father" of modern Morocco, preserved all the Moorish cities and built his European cities some miles apart from them. Thus the modern Fez of the twentieth century looks down from above on the old city, the Arab medina, dating back to the ninth and tenth centuries, and beyond well-shaded, well-watered gardens, on an offshoot of it, the "New Fez" of the thirteenth century. This comprises the grounds of the Sultan's Palace, and beyond its walls a quarter once reserved for the Jews and known as the Mellah. The name means "salt," and was derived from one of the traditional occupations of the Jews of Morocco, that of salting corpses—also of salting, in the bad old days, the heads which the Sultans chopped off their enemies, and of preparing them for public display on the walls, as it were *"pour encourager les autres."*

Fez is a city looking in on itself rather than out on the world, a self-centred city, like so many other Moslem holy places, but with a longer and more varied history than any other in North Africa. It is a maze of a city, with narrow winding streets and hardly a window looking onto them. For the old houses, many of them big family dwellings, are built onto court-yards. But it is a hive of human activity, particularly in the quarters devoted to the various trades and crafts. The liveliest is the bazaar of the brassworkers and coppersmiths, hammering out trays and bowls and all kinds of metal-work, in a pandemonium of sound. The blacksmiths and the carpenters and the shoemakers compete with them for noise and activity. Quieter are the bazaars of the tailors, the leatherworkers, the carpetmakers, the linen drapers, the silk merchants, the jewellers. Sweetest-smelling are the scent and the spice markets. Brightest-coloured is the quarter of the dyers, where great skeins of yarn are stirred in pots of brilliant reds and blues and yellows, staining the arms and the torsos of the dyers, who afterwards hang the skeins up to dry in the rafters. Down by the river the water wheels turn, grinding corn as they have done since the Middle Ages.

We are fortunate enough to have a long and detailed description of Fez in these times by a sixteenth-century writer named Leo Africanus—a Moslem from Spain who spent much of his youth in the city and afterwards travelled extensively. Captured by European pirates off Tunis, he was induced to adopt the Christian faith. He escaped sale in the slave market to be presented to Pope Leo X, baptized with his name, and educated under his patronage. He describes the life that went on in these bazaars and throughout the city in general, which had all the institutions of a kind of medieval welfare state.

There were well-endowed hospitals for the local population, and some "for sick and diseased strangers," who were given free food but had to pay for their own medicines. As Leo puts it, "certain women there are which attend upon them, till they recover their former health, or die." There were places "for frantic or distraught persons"—otherwise madhouses. The madmen were bound in chains, and when the governor brought them their food, he carried a whip "to chastise those that offer to bite, strike, or play any mad part." They used to shout at the passers-by, insisting that they were perfectly sane and were being unjustly detained. But if a sympathizer came near them, they would fling dung at him and plaster his face and his clothes with it.

There were, Leo tells us, a hundred public baths, with rooms of varying degrees of heat—like the Roman baths at Volubilis more than a thousand years before, and the Turkish baths to come, for the cleansing of later generations. The stoves that heated them were stoked, resourcefully, with dung-fuel, collected by boys from the stables all over the city, and dried in the sun. There were two hundred inns. All of them had fountains and water pipes and sinks, in the interests of cleanliness. But they afforded "beggarly entertainment to strangers," who had no beds or couches to lie on, but only a mat and a coarse blanket. The innkeepers belonged all to one tribe, and they had the unusual custom of dressing like women, shaving their beards, affecting feminine speech, and even, so Leo tells us, sometimes sitting down to spin. He goes on to tell us that they all had their female concubines, who were "not only ill-favoured in countenance but notorious for their bad life and behaviour."

There was, however, a more important side to Fez. For it was, above all things, a centre of culture and scholarship, a university city with a foundation earlier than most and superior to many in western Europe during these early Middle Ages. As the centuries passed and one dynasty succeeded another, Fez remained always the cultural if not always the political capital of Morocco. The university, the Qarawiyn Mosque, whose origins derive from the Holy City of Kairouan in Tunisia, was devoted largely to religious studies, to the teaching of Moslem theology, law, and kindred subjects, which still form the bulk of its curriculum. But it turned some attention to such scientific subjects as mathematics, geography, and astronomy, and through its academic prestige attracted scholars from all parts of the Moslem world.

In the process it accumulated a remarkable library, and it was regarded as a tragedy by Moslems when, in the seventeenth century, three thousand of its Arabic manuscripts and books, being transported from one Atlantic port to another, were captured by Christian pirates and transported to Spain. Here they were deposited in the Escorial at Madrid, and a large number of them burned when the palace was destroyed by fire. Nevertheless, Moulay Ismail, the great seventeenth-century Sultan of Morocco, was still able to leave behind him a library of twelve thousand volumes, which were distributed after his death among the various mosques and schools in the country. These schools, called in Arabic *medersas* and used, like monasteries, for both study and prayer, gather around the parent university mosque.

These places of learning and worship, which so enrich the architecture of the city of Fez, were built and decorated through the centuries in a succession of styles. Their predominant style is the Hispano-Mauresque, a blend of Spanish and Moorish, which flourished from the eleventh century onwards with the increasing settlement, in North Africa, of Moslems from Andalusia and their employment by the enlightened Almoravid dynasty. The Qarawiyn Mosque, as it exists today, is largely the work of Andalusian architects and craftsmen, who, for the first time since the Roman period but in their own very different idiom, endowed Morocco with buildings of lasting distinction, emulating more robustly such masterpieces as the great mosque of Cordova and the Alhambra at Granada. It was enlarged in the twelfth and thirteenth centuries to its present vast dimensions, consisting of sixteen aisles with twenty-one bays, all on arches with columns, a great expanse of green tiled roofs, space to hold more than twenty thousand people, and outside walls pierced by fourteen doorways, making a circuit of hardly less than a mile.

The schools, with their courtyards and fountains and cells for the students, date mostly from the fourteenth century, when the Hispano-Mauresque style was in full flower, growing more and more Spanish in feeling but still sobered down by the Moslems to create a nice synthesis of austerity and elegance, of simple architectural forms with rich decorative motifs. These prevail in the doors, inset with bronze panels in a filigree pattern; in the ceilings and lintels and panelling carved from the cedarwood of the Atlas Mountains; in columns and arches with delicate plasterwork, in elaborate texts of flowing Arab calligraphy treated as ornament; in the free use of marble, which the Arabs imported from Italy. Above all, there is a profusion of coloured tiles, in either floral or geometrical patterns, and often of a pure

Street scene in the medina, Taroudant

ABOVE: Women goat herders, Goulimine. RIGHT: Tower
of Almohad Hassan, twelfth century, unfinished, Rabat

turquoise blue, matching that of the heavens and thus often used to face the minarets of the mosques, towering heavenwards. The rulers of Fez valued their craftsmen and spared no expense in embellishing their buildings. One of the finest is the Bu Inania medersa, whose founder, the Emir Abu Inan, remarked when faced with the bill for it: "That which is beautiful is never dear, however great the sum; nothing is too much to buy that which pleases man."

Contrasting with Fez is the neighbouring and more open city of Meknes, chosen as his capital at the end of the seventeenth and beginning of the eighteenth century by Moulay Ismail, an all-powerful, tyrannical Sultan of the Alawite dynasty. He had a mania for building and devoted most of his reign to the creation, in the grand manner, of a palace and gardens designed to rival those of Versailles, which was being built at this time. He became a figure of international renown, or at least notoriety, a kind of Barbarian *grand seigneur*, who made alliances with the powers of Europe and even sought the hand of an illegitimate daughter of Louis XIV in marriage. He employed thirty thousand prisoners and twenty-five thousand Christian slaves on his building operations, and made it his practice, so tradition relates, to let no day pass without killing a few of them with his own hand—spearing a slave or two for sport as he went round the sites, nonchalantly chopping off heads as he rode down the ranks of his Black Guards, and building the bodies of his victims into the walls.

He had the reputation of keeping a human stud farm near Meknes, where he mated his Black Guardsmen with Negro women and also bred half-castes. It was written of him that "he always yokes his best-complexioned subjects to a black helpmate: and the fair lady must take up with a Negro. . . . Thus he takes care to lay the foundation of his tawny nurseries." Little of his palace now stands but its fortress walls, for his death led to a long period of anarchy and destruction. But the ruins of its buildings, more Spanish than Moroccan in style, survive over a wide area, overshadowing the rest of the city with their cumbersome walls and elaborate gateways.

The Alawites still rule over Morocco today, in the person of King Hassan II. Meanwhile Fez, between the founders, the Idrisids, and the Alawites, has known, over six hundred years, a sequence of four other imperial dynasties. All of them, unlike the Idrisids from the Arab East, originated in the Berber deep South, those lands of Morocco smelling of Africa which came to be the

29

OPPOSITE: Arab guarding gate in Rabat

cradle of its successive ruling people. The first to unite the whole country, north and south, were the Almoravids of the eleventh and early twelfth centuries—a nomadic Berber people, known as the Sanhaja. In the twelfth century they were supplanted by the Almohads, who ruled for a century and were supplanted in their turn by the Merinids, another nomad Saharan people. After two centuries they were followed by the Saadians, from a valley of the Saharan south, who ruled until the middle of the seventeenth century. Throughout these centuries Morocco was governed largely from the southern capital of Marrakesh, alternatively or concurrently with the northern capital of Fez.

From one capital to the other, from Fez southwards to Marrakesh across the great range of the Middle Atlas, there runs what is known as the "Sultan's Way." It winds upwards through cedar forests where Hannibal, the Carthaginian general, is supposed to have recruited his elephants. Strabo tells a tale that while other animals fled from a forest fire in these parts, the elephants stood their ground and fought the flames, to save the forests. He also records that the Romans made their tables, all in one piece, from the trunk of a single cedar tree. Beyond the watershed a new land reveals itself, the land of southern Morocco. A great red plain, with red villages, spreads westwards to the Atlantic and southwards towards the Sahara, with the High Atlas, Morocco's third and highest range of mountains, towering above it, some forty miles off, to a height of 12,000 feet. Spread over the edge of the plain is the city of Marrakesh.

Marrakesh, which wanders among palm groves, is the antithesis of Fez. For all its eight miles of ramparts, it is a city looking out upon the world rather than in on itself. It is an African city, a caravan city, a great market-place and a place of business and pleasure for the tribesmen coming in from the mountains around and the nomads coming in from the desert. It resembles in a sense an African encampment, whose inhabitants live not in tents but in houses and streets and bazaars. So it first was, when the nomadic Sanhaja in the eleventh century surged up from the south to make a fortified camp here and thus keep a vigilant eye on the Berbers settled in the mountains above. The Sanhaja were veiled men of the desert, like Tuareg, drinkers of camel-milk, eaters of camel-flesh, wearers of camel-hair. Familiar with means of irrigation in the Saharan oases, they dug artificial underground channels to bring water from the hills and so plant and fertilize the palm groves,

30

which still shade Marrakesh. They were a tribe of monastic warriors, waging a Holy War to spread the gospel of Islam, which had inspired one of their leaders in the course of a pilgrimage to the Holy Places of Mecca and Medina. Founding the Almoravid dynasty, they united not merely Morocco but Moslem Spain, giving it a new lease of life at a moment in history when its kingdoms were hard-pressed by the Christians. After the fall of Cordova and Toledo the King of Seville called in the strong arm of these Moroccan Berbers to his rescue, remarking, "I would rather be a camel-herd in Africa than a swine-herd in Castile." The strong arm was that of Yusuf ibn Tashfin, who thus brought glory to his dynasty and beauty to the cities of Morocco as of Spain.

It is to the succeeding dynasty of the Almohads that Marrakesh owes its supreme monument, the minaret of the Kutubia Mosque. A tower of warm red sandstone, honeycombed with intricate and delicate patterns in brick-work and with a frieze of dazzling white and turquoise tiles, it soars two hundred feet as though to compete with the heights of the Atlas, command-ing the city spread beneath it with a serene, glowing grace. Like the unfin-ished Hassan Tower at Rabat, it is the prototype of the Giralda Tower at Seville—worthy monuments both of an empire which stretched from the frontiers of Christian Europe right down to the fringe of the Sahara and Black Africa beyond. The mosque beneath it, according to the customs of Moslems on occupying a new city, was the first building to be erected in Marrakesh, and the ruler in person, with pious humility, tucked up his skirts with the rest of the workmen to mix the mud to make bricks for it, as the Prophet himself had done when building the first mosque in Medina.

Only one other important building of these early centuries in Marrakesh survives—the Kasbah mosque, and this, too, has a fine minaret, built of brick, with bright blue and white tiles. But from the thirteenth to the fifteenth centuries, under the Merinid dynasty, the city was eclipsed once more by Fez. Then in the sixteenth century there arose in Marrakesh a new dynasty, that of the Saadians, under Sultan Mansur, who sought to revive its glories and for a time succeeded in doing so. Resisting Christian encroachment, he ejected the Portuguese, who were making serious inroads into the country. But he made trade agreements with Britain and other Western powers, and a letter survives which he wrote to Queen Elizabeth. He turned his attention also to the Negro peoples in the south, mounting a military expedition in which he reached the River Niger and captured Timbuktu. He returned laden not only with a horde of black captives, but with a haul of gold ingots and other precious commodities, which won him the name of the "Golden Sultan."

Much of his wealth was spent in beautifying Marrakesh, where he built the immense El Badi Palace, employing foreign stonemasons and importing marble from Tuscany. An Arab poet praised it for "the perfumed soil, the glorious prospect and the lofty towers . . . the glory of Marrakesh and its pride." But the Sultan's fool, asked for his opinion, replied, "Well, Master, it'll make a big heap of rubble when it's demolished." And so it proved. For less than a century after Mansur's death it was razed to the ground by the jealous Moulay Ismail, the Alawite Sultan, who removed many of its materials to build his own palace at Meknes. Thus it survives only as a great relic, like a kind of ruined Alhambra, the open space within its bare walls converted each year into an arena for a festival of Berber dancing. But the tombs of the Saadian dynasty were not destroyed. They were only bricked up. They remained forgotten until the French unearthed them, soon after their occupation of Marrakesh. Thus they survive intact, giving an idea of the somewhat mixed but still elegant architectural style of the "Golden Sultan."

But the charm of this city among palm groves lies less in its monuments than in the streets of its Kasbah, and particularly in its huge African market-place, the Jemaa el-Fna. It is a wide-open space seething with life, no longer that of a slave market, as it once was, but of a market for every imaginable kind of local produce. Above all, it is a place of entertainment, as it has always been, not only for the people of Marrakesh but for a large floating population of Berber tribesmen, from the surrounding mountains and deserts. Here are snake-charmers, sword-swallowers and fire-eaters, acrobats and conjurers, fortune-tellers, clowns, and performing monkeys. Here are whirling, swaying Berber dancers, including the boy dancers of the Chleuch, with painted faces. Here are story-tellers, holding circles of children and indeed adults entranced with their tales.

The life of these southern Berber people flourishes chiefly in the High Atlas, the great range of mountains which rides across the plain to the south of the city. Throughout its history this was a country so turbulent that it was not safely accessible to the foreigner until after the First World War, when the French authorities, who had been engaged in its pacification since 1912, finally brought it under control. Scattered throughout the range, on its spurs and in its valleys, are its kasbahs, or castles, battlemented villages with high towers, which seem to spring naturally from the red stone and sun-dried clay of this highland landscape—much as the Berbers themselves, natural and vigorous and direct in their gaze and demeanour, seem to be creatures of the earth which has borne them. These villages served the tribesmen as fortresses from which to fight one another and the central authority right into the twentieth century. Some of them were built by Moulay Ismail himself, the great Sultan of Meknes, in an unsuccessful attempt to hold down these rebellious subjects. But when the strong arm was withdrawn, they became strongholds for the guerrilla activities of the "robber barons" themselves. These resembled the clansmen of the Scottish Highlands before the last of the Jacobite rebellions in 1745—and even their names had a Scottish ring, the M'Touggi, for example, as it might be the McTavish.

The great chieftains were warlords of the Atlas, living often in castles of barbaric splendour, engaged in a struggle for power with one another, in a series of alliances with their neighbours. They exacted a ruinous tribute from unfriendly tribes, weakening them on the principle that, as one of them put it, an "empty sack" cannot stand upright. The last of these great medieval potentates—comparable to one of the belligerent barons of the Wars of the Roses in England—was the Glawi, Thami al-Glawi, the Pasha of Marrakesh, who was backed by the French in their policy of dividing and ruling Morocco, and used by them to help depose the father of the present Sultan, Mohammed V, in 1953. But a few years later, when Morocco received her independence, Mohammed was recalled from exile, and the Glawi died dispossessed of his power, his lands, and his fortune.

His former feudal castle, now in the hands of the Moroccan Government, commands, like an eagle's lair, the more easterly of the two main passes, across the High Atlas from Marrakesh, the Tizi-n'Tichka. Dominating the village of the Glawi's clan, Telouet, it is a labyrinthine mass of buildings, built and decorated in modern times but in the style of the Middle Ages, which suited the nature of his régime. The last great Berber stronghold in Moroccan history, it remains, thanks to the unhappy irony of his fall, still unfinished. Such is the sad end to a modern story of the Arabian—or, more literally, Barbarian—Nights.

The castle looks down over the southern slopes of the range into a dusty, sun-baked landscape, already Saharan in character. Here, amid palm groves spreading away to the fringe of the desert, is the town of Ouarzazate, which stands at the head of the palm-fringed valley of the River Dra, the nomadic homeland of the Saadian dynasty. Nearby is the labyrinthine Kasbah of Taourirt, and to the south-east looms the line of a lower mountain range, the Sarro, the last region to be pacified by the French, not long before the Second World War.

Across the more westerly of the two passes, the dramatic Tizi-n'Test, the road winds down into a contrasting fertile region, the steamy valley of the River Sous, which rises in the High Atlas and runs west into the Atlantic. Here in a semi-tropical landscape stands Taroudant, a rose-red fortified city within crenellated ramparts, which flourished through successive dynasties from the eleventh century onwards and was at periods the capital of an independent Berber principality. In the sixteenth century it was a prosperous centre of the sugar trade. Queen Elizabeth's household is said to have consumed 18,000 pounds of Moroccan sugar in a single year, in exchange for which the Moroccans imported English timber for shipbuilding, and arms, while sugar was traded with the Italians for marble. Plantations of sugar cane flourish still in the Sous valley, among grainfields and orchards and olive groves.

To the south it is bounded by the Anti-Atlas, Morocco's final mountain range. Among its foothills is Tafraout, an idyllic village set amid olive and almond and palm trees, with a romantic landscape of pink granite crags soaring above and around it. The road from it leads down to the Atlantic coast at Tiznit, a fort built in the 1880s by the Sultan Moulay Hassan, in his efforts to suppress the Berbers of the Sous valley and the Anti-Atlas range. It was the French authorities who eventually did so, in 1917, deposing a rebel, El Hiba, who had ruled here for five years as a Pretender to the Sultanate. The inhabitants of the region survive—or fail to survive—largely through a process described as "agricultural poker." This takes the form of gambling on rainfall. One year, or possibly two years out of three, it will rain and their barley crop will ripen. In the third year it will not, and they will be left with nothing. But the region breeds resourceful Berber craftsmen, for whom the sale of rough silver jewellery ekes out a living denied by the heavens.

South of Tiznit is Goulimine, the "end of the road" before the Sahara takes over—first a region whose river normally dries up before it reaches the Atlantic, then the Spanish Sahara, all that now remains to Spain, besides the enclave of Ifni, from wide imperial claims in southern Morocco. Gouli-mine was once a caravan centre, linked with Timbuktu. Today it comes to life each week as a Berber market, to which tribesmen and their women and children flock in from the surrounding deserts, picturesquely garbed and including among them the nomadic "Blue People" of the veil, who are akin to the Tuareg. In the evenings, around camp fires, they dance their traditional dances, before the caravans trek back into the desert in the cool of the night.

Northwards from here to the Straits of Gibraltar stretch some seven hundred miles of Atlantic coast-line. Most of its harbours during the fourteenth and fifteenth centuries were occupied as trading posts by the Portuguese, who levied a heavy tribute on rival Spanish, French, and Genoese traders. This foreign occupation, in the guise of a protectorate, brought commercial profit to the Moroccans, but aroused in them an increasing political and religious resentment, which led ultimately to the ejection of the Portuguese by the Saadian dynasty. Their most southerly port was Agadir, the natural outlet for the Sous valley, which they named Santa Cruz de Aguer. It reappeared in international history in 1911 when the Germans, pursuing African colonial ambitions in competition with the French, threatened to dispatch a gunboat to Agadir, an incident which, but for diplomatic British action, might have precipitated a world war three years before its actual outbreak. In 1960, converted meanwhile into a holiday resort, Agadir and much of its hinterland were destroyed, with immense casualties, in an earthquake, a disaster from which it was not to recover for almost a decade.

As a trading centre it had been supplanted by Mogador, a port farther up the Atlantic coast, overlooking an offshore island where Sir Francis Drake made his first landfall on his round-the-world journey from Plymouth on Christmas Day, 1577. Once a Portuguese station, it is today a stone-walled city, built, to compete with Agadir, by Mohammed III, an Alawite Sultan of the eighteenth century. He employed European architects to design it, one a Frenchman said to be his prisoner, and the other an Englishman, converted to Islam and known as Ahmed el-Inglizi—otherwise Ahmed the Englishman. Covering a small peninsula which is almost an island, Mogador has been described as a kind of "European fantasy on a Moroccan theme." In fact, in its style it is essentially a product of the European eighteenth century, its streets laid out in a symmetrical classical manner and enclosed within battlements, broad and streamlined and broken by semicircular bastions. For two hundred years it was inhabited largely by Jews, merchants who handled its trade with the advantage of customs concessions. But the creation of the State of Israel caused their departure and its reversion, with a predominantly Berber population, to the Arab name of Essaouira.

Northwards again up the coast is the port of Safi. Here a sixteenth-century Portuguese castle encloses the remains of a late Berber palace and overlooks those of an earlier fortified monastery, where the warriors of the Islamic faith resisted Christian incursions. Beyond the medina is a market renowned for its local bright-coloured pottery. Otherwise Safi becomes an increasingly industrial port, through the development of natural phosphates, derived from its hinterland and worked in a chemical plant to become a major export for modern Morocco. Next up the coast is Mazagan, now known by its Arab name of El Jadida, and remarkable chiefly for a large underground vaulted cistern, built by the Portuguese for the storage of water in the sixteenth century.

Thus Casablanca is reached, Morocco's great modern industrial city developed under the French protectorate, whose population has since risen to more than a million. Casablanca is the commercial, as Rabat, to the north of it, is the political capital of Morocco today. The port of Rabat, lying just across its Bou Regreg estuary, is Salé, a place historically associated less with the Portuguese than with the Spaniards, for whom this northern Atlantic coast-line and the Mediterranean coasts beyond were a natural orbit of aggression and ultimate expansion. They seized and sacked Salé in the thirteenth century, but on its recapture it developed, under the Merinids, into an important Moroccan mercantile centre, trading with the Christian powers of the Mediterranean, Britain, and Flanders. In the seventeenth century it was settled by a large community of Moorish refugees, expelled from Spain after the final reconquest by the Christians, who became known as the Moriscos.

Forcibly converted meanwhile from the Moslem to the Christian faith, they hardly knew what they were, but saw themselves still as Andalusians and thus fell between two powers. Overflowing across into Rabat, which became known as New Salé, they established for themselves the small Republic of Bou Regreg, which subsisted through piracy. As privateers, taking their revenge upon Spain for their expulsion and on the Christian powers in general for their inroads on Morocco, they attacked Christian shipping in

ABOVE: Entrance gate to Chella, Rabat. OVER-
LEAF: Sanctuary of the Merinids, Chella, Rabat

Fourteenth-century *qubba* in Chella, Rabat

the Atlantic, including argosies from the New World, and raided the south coast of England, where they became notorious as the "Sally Rovers." It was they who, in Defoe's story, captured Robinson Crusoe, whom they brought into Salé through a gate still associated with his name.

These privateers operated largely from the Oudaia Kasbah, commanding the ocean and the mouth of the Bou Regreg River from the northern point of Rabat. Its name is derived from the Oudaia tribesmen, people from the remote southern Sahara whom the Sultans employed as troops, largely for garrison duties, on the grounds that they were unlikely to forge alliances with the native tribes around them. Before its "Pirates' Tower" there spreads today a fragrant shaded garden, laid out and planted in the Andalusian manner under the auspices of Marshal Lyautey, the French "ruler" of Morocco, who made Rabat its capital in 1912—restoring the old monuments of its medina and building a new city apart from it, in a modern Moorish style. Rabat derived its name from *ribat*, an Arabic word for "stronghold" or "safe anchorage," and was at one time known as Ribat-el-Fath, the "camp of victory." It was founded, probably on the site of the Oudaia Kasbah, in the tenth century, as a fortified monastery of the Orthodox Islamic faith, built to combat the fanatical and powerful warriors of heretic Berber tribes.

Later, in the twelfth century, it became a great city of the Almohads, said to have been built by Spanish Christian slaves, who were afterwards settled as freemen in the mountain region east of Fez, and eventually became absorbed in both language and religion into the Berber tribes around them. Leo Africanus described it as "exceedingly beautified" by its builders, "with temples, colleges, palaces, shops, stores, hospitals, and other such buildings," and above all by a high tower "from the top whereof they might escrie ships an huge way into the sea." This is the Hassan Tower, built of glowing red stone, higher than its counterparts, the Kutubia at Marrakesh and the Giralda at Seville, with an interior ramp so broad that, according to Leo, "three horses abreast might well go up." As minaret of the adjoining Hassan Mosque, it was designed by its builder, Sultan Yaqub el-Mansur, to become a famous place of Moslem pilgrimage, celebrating his great victory over the Christians at the Battle of Alarcos in Spain in 1195. But he died only four years later. The tower was never completed, and the mosque now lies in ruins. Replacing them is a new shrine, built at great cost by the present King Hassan of Morocco as a mausoleum for his father, Sultan Mohammed V, and representing a modern apotheosis of all that is most lavish and elaborate in the Hispano-Mauresque style. Thus, through a sequence of dynasties, does historical and architectural continuity prevail in Morocco as in no other North African country.

The Sultans of its Merinid dynasty he buried in seclusion beyond the walls of Rabat, within a walled necropolis approached through a castellated gateway as massive as that of a fortress. This is at Chella, the site of a maritime station of the Romans, and probably of the Phoenicians before them, which bore the name of Sala Colonia. According to Pliny its neighbourhood, that of the most southerly Roman settlement in Morocco, was infested with elephants, which have long since disappeared, and with recalcitrant tribesmen, whose descendants presumably survive. From its rose-red ramparts a path descends to a spring, once channelled into a fountain for religious ablutions, now watering a profuse garden of palms and olives, flowering shrubs and fruit trees. Today only the excavated site of the Roman town remains, with a few scattered architectural fragments. But the Islamic necropolis preserves still in its tombs and its ruins the charm and the atmosphere of Morocco's fourteenth-century past.

To the accompaniment of murmuring waters, the trees refresh with their fragrance and shade with their branches the graves of the Sultans and the ruins of their places of worship, where a crumbling minaret stands, glowing with honeycombed stone patterns and scintillant tilework, and the storks build their nests in its tower. Among the tombs is that of the mother of the Merinid Sultan abu Inan, named "Morning Sun," who had been a slave and thus doubtless a Christian. It bears the inscription, "Praise be to God! This is the grave of our lady, the noble, pure, devout and saintly mother of the Sultan, Khalifa and Imam . . . Our Lord, Commander of the Faithful, the reliant on the Lord of the Worlds, Abu Inan. . . . May God install her in the fullness of his heaven and receive her with indulgence and pardon." The inscription shows that this line of Sultans used the title of Caliph, to which they were not by heredity entitled, within their own dominions.

The medina, the old Moorish town of Rabat, is bounded on the north and east sides by the sea and the estuary, on the west by the Almohad Wall, built in the twelfth century and pierced by five monumental gateways, and on the south by the Andalusian Wall. This dates from the period of the Moriscos, who probably built most of the medina. Among its inhabitants Spanish surnames still survive. A flavour of the Spanish Renaissance persists in the style of arches and fountains and the ornamentation of doorways.

Similar patterns are repeated in the local embroidery, while wooden chests are still made to a design which is traditionally Spanish in origin. The medina is a hive of a town, with tortuous streets and lanes, often overhung by lattices and spanned by whitewashed vaults. One street is notably straight by comparison, the rue des Consuls, where all foreign representatives were obliged to live before the French occupation in 1912. The city which the French built, beyond its walls, reverts, by comparison on an imperial scale, to the classical symmetry of the Roman colonial outpost of Sala.

As the power of the Portuguese waned in Morocco, so did the power of the Spaniards grow. These northern Atlantic ports to the south of the Straits of Gibraltar, and the Mediterranean ports to the east of them, were a natural orbit for Spanish encroachment, which increased following the final collapse of Moslem rule in Spain at the end of the fifteenth century. North of Salé are Kenitra, which the French named Port Lyautey, and, close to it, the small Kasbah of Mehdia, which was garrisoned by the Spaniards during the seventeenth century, as a post from which to keep watch on the "Sally Rovers." Here originally was a Phoenician colony of Carthage, known as Thymaterium and dating back some centuries before the Roman colony of Sala. The Phoenicians, like the Portuguese after them, were adventurous navigators. Tradition claims that they penetrated as far as the Cape of Good Hope, thus forestalling Vasco da Gama by a thousand years, and from Thymaterium, as recorded by Hanno, they travelled southwards to Sierra Leone and beyond, encountering trouble towards the end of their journey with a tribe of hairy savages who were known, so they learned, as Gorillas.

An earlier Carthaginian settlement was on the site of the present Larache, an Atlantic port south of the Straits of Gibraltar—a channel running, in the eyes of the ancients, between the Pillars of Hercules. Larache, too, was occupied by the Spaniards in the seventeenth century, together with Azila to the north of it. Already, since the previous century, they had been established in the Mediterranean both at Ceuta, the southern Pillar of Hercules, and at Melilla, a port to the east of it, close to the Algerian frontier. Though unwelcome to the Moroccans, these annexations by the Spaniards were at least regarded as a lesser evil than the threat, at this time, of annexation by the Ottoman Turks. The Arabs of Algeria had made use of the Turks to eject the Spaniards, and now found themselves under Turkish rule. The Berbers of Morocco preferred to use the Spaniards as a counterweight to the Turks and thus found themselves free from them. They remained relatively free also from Spanish rule, at least in the interior, until the twentieth century when, under the Convention of 1912, Spain, from the bridgeheads of Larache, Ceuta, and Melilla, occupied much of northern Morocco to establish a Spanish protectorate, marching with that of the French. Only then did the Moroccans lose an independence which they had enjoyed for more than a thousand years—but which they were to enjoy once more half a century later.

The capital of the Spanish zone, matching the capital of the French zone at Rabat, was Tetouan, which has now reverted to Moroccan provincial status. Once it stood on an outlet to the sea, and in the sixteenth century served as a base for privateers, like Rabat, harbouring a group of those notorious Barbary Corsairs who, on the expulsion of the Moors from Spain, were the Mediterranean counterpart of the Atlantic "Sally Rovers." But Philip II of Spain took his revenge on them by blocking their harbour, now no more than a silted river mouth beneath hillsides of orchards and olive groves. Thenceforward they were outclassed along the Barbary coast by their piratical brethren in Algeria, Tunisia, and Tripoli, who, under Turkish protection and leadership, controlled the Mediterranean for more than three centuries, raiding and levying tribute on the merchant fleets of a disunited Christian Europe. Lacking the harbour for large vessels, the Moors of Tetouan could play little part in this brigandage. Nonetheless, with their small galleys they became a nuisance to Spanish interests in Ceuta, and in 1860 Spain captured and occupied Tetouan, withdrawing after two years on payment of a large indemnity by the Sultan, and returning only in 1913. They made of it, within crenellated stone walls and overflowing beyond them, a white city of charm, graceful in ornament and wholly Andalusian in character, recalling Cordova or some other city of Spain.

Up in the hills behind Tetouan is Chaouen, a small town sacred to an early Moslem saint, to which infidels, until the present century, seldom dared penetrate for fear of death. An adventurous young Spaniard reached it in 1863, but was never seen again. Twenty years later a saintly Christian, Charles de Foucauld, who was to become a great French explorer, contrived to spend a night in its Jewish quarter, the Mellah, but was spat upon by the Moslems, who cursed, "May God eternally burn the father that begot thee, Jew, son of a Jew."

When the Spaniards first occupied Chaouen in 1920, they were welcomed by its Jews, who, harking back to the dynastic Spain of the fifteenth century, cried out to the soldiery, "Viva Isabella!" Today the Islamic severity of Chaouen is tempered by Spanish taste and an eye for the picturesque in colour-washed houses and brightly tiled roofs, and by an atmosphere of *douceur de vivre* which belongs essentially to the Christian Mediterranean. A large welcoming village, it looks no longer in on itself but out on the world from the rigid embrace of a circle of mountains towering above and around it. These are the mountains of the Rif, Morocco's northernmost range and the last of its barriers to yield to the foreigner.

In 1921 there arose in these mountains a redoubtable Berber rebel, Abd el-Krim, who raised their tribes, drove the Spaniards back to the coast, and proclaimed himself President of an independent Rif Republic, perhaps the last all-Berber state in history. For five years he waged guerrilla warfare against the forces of Spain, finally declaring a Holy War against Christians in general. He marched against the French and sent raiding bands almost as far as the gates of Fez, where he aspired to proclaim himself Sultan. This united the French and Spanish forces against him and thus led to his defeat and exile, enabling the Spaniards to complete the pacification of their zone and establish with the Moroccans a relationship which proved to be easier than that of the French. It was from Melilla, Tetouan, Ceuta, and Larache that in 1936 General Franco, landing from the Canary Islands, rallied the Moroccan garrisons in the anti-Republican risings which launched the Spanish Civil War. History had come round full circle. It was a little over twelve centuries since the Moors themselves, from here, had invaded Spain.

The first Arab invader of Morocco, Uqba, had looked only westwards, reaching the Atlantic, riding his horse into the ocean until the water was up to its neck, and then, runs the legend, crying out to Allah, "O God, I take you to witness that there is no ford here. If there were, I would cross!" The next invader, a generation later, looked northwards across the Straits to Europe. As Hannibal had done before him, he invaded Spain, with the support of Berber troops, under a Berber general named Tarik, giving his name to the rock, Gebel Tarik, which he captured and which we now know as Gibraltar. The base for this invasion was Tangier, a port in the Straits commanding the point where the Mediterranean meets the Atlantic. Traditionally founded by Hercules and known to the ancients as Tingi, glorified by legend, according to Leo Africanus, as an "earthly paradise" with walls of brass and roofs of gold and silver; apostrophized in the Middle Ages by Saint Francis of Assisi as Tingis, the demented, deluded city, Tangier has had a long and varied international history and can claim to be the oldest continuously inhabited city in Morocco. The Portuguese captured it in the fifteenth century, converting its mosques into churches. After a period of Spanish rule, it was ceded by Portugal to England in 1661, as part of the dowry of the Infanta Catherine of Braganza, on her marriage to Charles II.

The English built a jetty and a fort for seaward and also for landward defence against the hostile Alawite Sultan Moulay Ismail. Outmanœuvred by the Moors and finding its occupation too costly, they held Tangier for little more than twenty years. Finally, to the satisfaction of the Sultan, it was evacuated under Parliament's orders, on the grounds mainly that it was an economic liability, but ostensibly that its garrison "might be exposed to the taint of Popery." Samuel Pepys visited the city at this time, in his capacity as an Admiralty official, to advise Lord Dartmouth, Admiral of the Fleet, on the evacuation of Tangier and the demolition of its fortifications. Pepys found "nothing but vice in the whole place of all sorts, for swearing, cursing, drinking and whoring." He observed that "the greatest part, if not the whole, use of the hospital is for rogues and jades that have the pox," that "the women of the town are, generally speaking, whores," and that the Governor "is said to have got his wife's sister with child, and that while he is with his whores at his little bathing house which he has furnished with a jade a purpose for that use there, his wife, whom he keeps in awe, sends for her gallants and plays the jade herself at home." Thanks to Lord Dartmouth's destruction—for which he received a personal grant of £10,000 from a grateful English Government—the best part of Tangier, including the mole which made of it a serviceable harbour, was left largely in ruins.

Afterwards it was to grow, nonetheless, into a lively cosmopolitan city, thronged with merchants, Moroccan, Jewish, and European, from such countries as Spain, France, and Holland. It became more so in the course of the nineteenth century, with the increase of foreign investments and the growth of a large Consular community. In 1912 it was officially acknowledged to have a "special character," and this, in 1923, was confirmed by a "Statute of Tangier," involving a Committee of Control composed of the Consuls of the various powers; economic equality for all of them; neutralization; and Mixed Courts with European judges replacing the former Consular Courts —all under the ultimate authority of the Sultan, whom an agent represented.

This international régime persisted after the Second World War (following a period of Spanish occupation in the course of it) with the inclusion of the United States and, in theory, Soviet Russia, bringing a boom to Tangier through the influx of traders, financiers, and speculators. This lasted until 1960, when it reverted to Morocco and fell into a state of depression, now relieved by an influx of tourists.

Tangier still embodies the familiar components of a Moroccan city—medina with Kasbah, Sultan's Palace, mosques, and bazaars, called the Grand and the Petit Socco, a name derived from the Spanish *zocco* meaning "souk" or "market." At the summit of the town, approached by steps, overlooking both the Atlantic and the Mediterranean, is the Kasbah Square, a quarter still Moorish in character and relatively free from modern European buildings. On this site once stood the "Upper Castle," built as a headquarters by the English, above a fort which came to be known as York Castle, in honour of the Duke of York. Destroyed on their evacuation, it was rebuilt by the Moroccans soon afterwards, and a part of it became the palace, little used, of a succession of Sultans.

Tangier, however, remains in its atmosphere an international city. Unlike other cities of Morocco, looking inwards on themselves, southwards into Africa, or westwards to the Atlantic, it looks outwards and northwards towards Europe. It is the westerly outpost of that "Fourth Shore" of Europe spreading eastwards to Algeria, Tunis, and Tripoli, where, in 1942, the forces of Britain and America landed to invade and liberate its main shore, and so to save European civilization.

ABOVE: Interior view showing the decorative ivory stucco.
OPPOSITE: Small side street in the medina, Fez. OVERLEAF: Street
scene in the busy Attarin Souk, the commercial center of Fez

LEFT: The tanners' quarter in Fez. ABOVE: Street vendor of flowers and herbs, Fez

OVERLEAF: A general view of Marrakesh with the twelfth-century Kutubia minaret rising in the foreground

ABOVE: The Kutubia Mosque, built during the dynasty of the Almohads, especially noted for its minaret, which soars to a height of two hundred feet. OPPOSITE: The garden court at Dar Sidi Sa'id palace, now a museum of folk art

OVERLEAF: Folk dancers in Jemaa el Fna, main square of Marrakesh

OPPOSITE: Ancient gate leading into the Souk, Marrakesh. ABOVE: Basket weaver's shop in the Souk

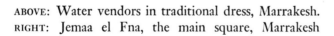

ABOVE: Water vendors in traditional dress, Marrakesh.
RIGHT: Jemaa el Fna, the main square, Marrakesh

ABOVE: Forecourt of the Merinid Medersa Yusufia in Marrakesh; noted as one of the most beautiful monuments in Morocco, also the largest Islamic college (sixteenth century). OPPOSITE AND OVERLEAF: Ceremonial dancers at the annual festival, Marrakesh

The rite of the "fantasia." An exhibition of exciting
and skillful horsemanship. This is most often the climax
of any festival or local celebration, as seen overleaf

ABOVE: Two noble Arab spectators at the festival.
OPPOSITE: Young Moroccan girl in festive dress

OPPOSITE: Almoravid *qubba*, al-Barudiyin (twelfth century) in Marrakesh.
This tomb was discovered as recently as 1948. ABOVE: View of the ceiling

ABOVE: Small fourteenth-century fort outside Marrakesh. RIGHT:
Typical archway gate leading into the Kasbah, Marrakesh

OVERLEAF: Stork nest complete with young, Ouarzazate.
In the far distance the snow-covered High Atlas Mountains

ABOVE: Old man in traditional peasant dress, Ouarzazate. RIGHT: Street scene in Ouarzazate

Women of Tinerhir at a marriage feast

OPPOSITE: Young Berber girl attending a wedding, wearing
fine handmade silver jewelry. ABOVE: Sheep herder, Goulimine

LEFT: Camel market at Goulimine. ABOVE:
The famous Girda dancers from Goulimine

OPPOSITE: The Tribunal building in Casablanca. ABOVE: Detail of the hand-carved cupola inside the Tribunal building

The great walls and ramparts of Chella, Rabat

ABOVE: Fourteenth-century gateway to Chella, the ancient
sanctuary of the Merinids. OPPOSITE: The new mosque
built by King Hassan, named after his father, Mohammed V

Market scene at Ceuta